KNIGHTS
OF THE
LUNCH TABLE

THE DODGEBALL CHRONICLES

by

FRANK CAMMUSO

001 XCL

graphix

AN IMPRINT OF

SCHOLASTIC

New York   Toronto   London   Auckland   Sydney   Mexico City   New Delhi   Hong Kong   Buenos Aires

This book is for anyone who has ever been picked last.
— FC

Special thanks to Ngoc Huynh, Hart Seely,
Phil McAndrew, Peter Allen, Tom Peyer, Michael Cho,
Bruce Coville, Michael and Harrison Jantze, Sheila
Keenan, Phil Falco, Janna Morishima, David Saylor, David
McCormick, all the fine folks at *The Post-Standard*
and especially the students, faculty, and staff of
Durgee Junior High School.

Library of Congress Cataloging-in-Publication Data

Cammuso, Frank.
The dodgeball chronicles / by Frank Cammuso. — 1st ed.
p. cm. — (Knights of the lunch table ; 1)
ISBN-13: 978-0-439-90322-6 (alk. paper)
ISBN-10: 0-439-90322-X (alk. paper)
1. Graphic novel. I. Title.
PN6727.C28D63 2008
741.5'973—dc22

2007037480

10 9 8 7 6 5 4 3 2   08 09 10

First edition, July 2008

Edited by Sheila Keenan
Creative Director: David Saylor
Book design by Phil Falco
Lettering by John Green
Printed in the U.S.A.

YOU DON'T . . .

YES I DO! I STINK AT BASEBALL, FOOTBALL AND *DODGEBALL!* I STINK AT EVERYTHING! ALL I WANT IS *TO BE GOOD* AT SOMETHING! *ANYTHING!*

WITH THAT COMBINATION YOU CAN SUCCEED AT ANYTHING.

EVEN DODGEBALL?

YOU ARE GOOD AT THINGS. YOU'RE SMART, CARING AND VERY BRAVE.

SURE. YOU COULD BECOME A DODGEBALL LEGEND IF YOU WANT.

REALLY?

REALLY. NOW, HOW ABOUT GETTING UP? THE BUS WILL BE HERE SOON.

YEAH, OK.

6

DON'T WORRY. BUSES ARE OVERRATED.

TO YOU MAYBE, BUT IT'S MY FIRST DAY AT A NEW SCHOOL.

OH, I SEE. WHAT IF I TOLD YOU I COULD MAGICALLY TRANSPORT YOU THERE?

YOU CAN?

NO, BUT I DO KNOW A SHORTCUT.

FOLLOW THAT PATH THROUGH THE WOODS AND YOU'LL BE TO SCHOOL IN TEN MINUTES.

YOU SURE?

I'M KINDA GOOD AT THIS GUIDANCE STUFF. AS A MATTER OF FACT, HERE'S A PREDICTION FOR YOU: THIS WEEK, YOU SHALL BE TESTED IN WAYS YOU'VE NEVER IMAGINED.

GEE, THANKS.

DON'T MENTION IT. SEE YA!

HOOOWWLL

WHAT'S THAT?!

WHAT'S *HE* DOING?

COOL! DOES HE BITE?

NAH, HANNIBAL JUST CHILLS. MY SCIENCE TEACHER, MR. MERLYN, ASKED ME TO BRING HIM IN.

I'M ARTIE!

PERCY. ACTUALLY, MY REAL NAME IS PERCIVAL, BUT PLEASE DON'T EVER CALL ME THAT, OK?

HOOWLLLL

THAT SOUNDED CLOSE.

YEAH, SO WE BETTER GET TO SCHOOL. IT'S GETTING LATE.

GGRRRRR

CHECK IT OUT! A *DODGEBALL!*

YEAH, THEY TAKE IT SERIOUSLY AROUND HERE. YOU PLAY?

UH, NO, I MEAN, *YEAH*.

BACK AT MY OLD SCHOOL, I WAS A *DODGEBALL LEGEND.* I WAS ALL-STATE, FIRST TEAM.

LUCKY YOU. I HATE DODGEBALL.

YOU DO?

IT'S PROBABLY HARD FOR YOU TO UNDERSTAND, BUT *NOT EVERYBODY* IS GOOD AT DODGEBALL.

UM, ACTUALLY, I WAS . . .

C'MON, THE COAST IS CLEAR, LET'S GET IN BEFORE *THE HORDE* SEES US.

THE HORDE? WHAT'S A *HORDE?*

SEE THOSE GUYS PLAYING DODGEBALL? THAT'S *THE HORDE*. THEY PUSH EVERYBODY AROUND. THEY TAKE OUR STUFF. THEY KINDA RULE THE SCHOOL.

C'MON, LET'S . . .

HEY, PERCIVAL, WHAT'S IN YOUR PURSE?

WHATCHA GOT FOR ME TODAY, PERCIVAL?

NOTHING.

IT DOESN'T LOOK LIKE *NOTHING*, PERCIVAL. YOU KNOW YOU GOTTA GIVE ME *SOMETHING* OR YOU CAN'T GET IN.

HERE, YOU CAN HAVE MY LUNCH.

WARTHE

THAT'LL WORK!

LATER, LADIES.

YOU DIDN'T HAVE TO DO THAT.

IT'S OK, MY SISTER PROBABLY SPIT IN IT ANYWAYS.

WHO WAS THAT?

DWAYNE FERRYMAN. HE'S WITH THE HORDE. THOSE JERKS SHAKE ME DOWN EVERY WEEK.

WHY DOESN'T THE PRINCIPAL DO SOMETHING ABOUT THEM?

PRINCIPAL DAGGER? ARE YOU KIDDING? SHE'S *WORSE*.

PLEASE, OH, PLEASE, MRS. DAGGER, *WISE AND POWERFUL QUEEN* OF THE SCHOOL. I BEG YOU. *PLEASE*, I'LL NEVER DO IT AGAIN!

STOP GROVELING, MR. KOZLOWSKI. YOU'RE GETTING SPITTLE ON MY SHOES!

YOU KNOW THE RULES. *NO* ELECTRONIC DEVICES ON SCHOOL GROUNDS. THANK YOU FOR YOUR *DONATION!*

BUT IT'S NOT MINE! IT'S MY BROTHER'S!

TOO BAD.

THAT STINKS!

PERHAPS, YOU'D LIKE TO FAMILIARIZE YOURSELF WITH THIS DURING LUNCH PERIOD DETENTION.

Camelot Middle School Rules and Regulations Vol. IX

RULES ARE RULES, MR. KOZLOWSKI. IF WE DIDN'T HAVE RULES, DO YOU KNOW WHAT WE'D HAVE?

FUN?

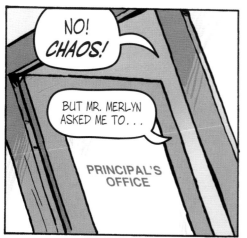

NO! *CHAOS!*

BUT MR. MERLYN ASKED ME TO . . .

PRINCIPAL'S OFFICE

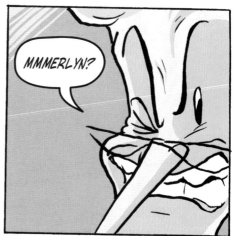

MMMERLYN?

SOME TEACHERS, LIKE MR. MERLYN, WOULD HAVE YOU BELIEVE THAT A SUCCESSFUL EDUCATION IS BASED ON FREEDOM, RESPECT AND UNDERSTANDING.

I'LL TELL YOU WHAT THAT'S A COMBINATION FOR . . . *FAILURE.*

EDUCATION MEANS *DISCIPLINE, CONTROL, FEAR* . . .

MRS. DAGGER, WHO ARE YOU TALKING TO?

MISS FLUNKE, I . . . ?!

IT'S TIME FOR MORNING ANNOUNCEMENTS, MA'AM.

YES, YES, OF COURSE.

19

NOBODY MESSES WITH . . .

JOSEPH ROMAN, WHAT'S GOING ON HERE?

HULLO, MRS. DAGGER.

I'M *SURPRISED* AT YOU, YOUNG MAN.

SORRY, MRS. DAGGER.

YOU SHOULD KNOW BETTER.

WHY AREN'T YOU BOYS PRACTICING DODGEBALL?

HANNIBAL?

I WANT YOU TO WIN THE DISTRICT TROPHY AGAIN.

I HAVE A VERY GOOD FEELING ABOUT THIS SEASON.

NO LONGER SHALL WE CRAWL IN THE LOWER DIVISIONS.

NO SIR, THIS TIME, *VICTORY* IS WITHIN OUR GRASP.

THIS YEAR THE MIGHTY WILL FALL . . .

YOU! IN MY OFFICE. *NOW!!*

YOU WANT ME TO *STEAL* IT??

SSHHHH! IT'S NOT STEALING! IT'S MORE LIKE *RETRIEVING.*

WHEN YOU GET IN THERE, I'LL GIVE YOU THE SIGNAL. JUST GRAB IT.

WHAT SIGNAL?

I KNEW I COULD COUNT ON YOU. LATER!

PIZZA PALA

UH! WAIT! WHERE ARE YOU GOING?

WHERE IS *WHO* GOING?

AND WHO ARE *YOU?* WHAT EDUCATIONAL BLACK HOLE SPIT YOU OUT AND BLESSED US WITH YOUR *WORMLIKE* PRESENCE?

MY NAME IS ARTHUR KING. I JUST MOVED FROM CORNWALL. I'M NEW.

YEAH. HOORAH. WONDERFUL. WE CERTAINLY ARE *LUCKY* HERE. LET'S SEE WHAT YOUR FILE SAYS.

HMMF, I SEE, YOU MUST BE SOOOO PROUD OF YOURSELF. *B-MINUS. B-MINUS. C-PLUS.* TELL ME, MR. KING, ARE YOU GOOD AT ANYTHING?

WELL, I'M . . .

THAT'S NOT A QUESTION. ≷SIGH≷

I DON'T KNOW HOW THEY DO THINGS OVER IN CORNWALL, BUT AT CAMELOT MIDDLE SCHOOL, WE OPERATE ON ONLY THE *HIGHEST* OF STANDARDS.

WE DO NOT TOLERATE CONNIVING LITTLE *WORMS* THAT GO AROUND SUBVERTING THE EDUCATIONAL PROGRAM AND ASSAULTING OUR FACULTY.

I'M SORRY, BUT IT WAS AN ACCIDENT.

SO YOU SAY. CONSIDER THIS *STRIKE ONE*. DO YOU HEAR ME? TWO MORE STRIKES, AND YOU'RE *OUT*. SUSPENSION. IS THAT UNDERSTOOD? VERY WELL, LUNCH PERIOD DETENTION FOR A WEEK! YOU'RE DIS . . .

UH, MA'AM? YOUR *TWENTY-SEVEN PEPPERONI PIZZAS* ARE HERE!

WHAT? I DIDN'T ORDER ANY PIZZAS!

I *HATE* PIZZA!

WHAT KIND OF FOOL ORDERS TWENTY-SEVEN PIZZAS AT NINE IN THE MORNING?

31

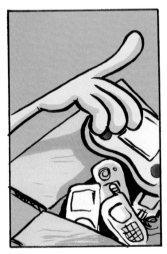

WHAT ARE YOU STILL DOING HERE?

UH, I DON'T HAVE A LOCKER YET, MA'AM.

A LOCKER, YOU SAY? *MISS FLUNKE,* WE MUST GIVE THIS FINE BOY A LOCKER!

MMM, THIS IS REALLY GOOD PIZZA. YOU SHOULD...

MISS FLUNKE, GIVE MR. KING LOCKER #001XCL.

YES, MA'AM, UH, THAT LOCKER IS...

IT HASN'T BEEN OPENED IN YEARS.

DON'T BE SILLY. GIVE MR. KING LOCKER #001XCL.

BUT...

GLADYS... GIVE... HIM... THE... LOCKER!

YES, MA'AM.

I WILL BE KEEPING AN EYE ON YOU, WORM. I KNOW WHAT YOU'RE UP TO. TWO MORE STRIKES, AND YOU'RE OUT. *TWO MORE.*

WHERE'S HE GOING?

I GOT YOU NOW!

TOMATO SOUP

BANANAS BUNCH

WHO APPROACHES THE LADIES' LUNCH?

MY NAME IS ARTIE, I THINK I'M LOST.

BEANS OF GREEN

STICKS OF FISH

TELL US, CHILD. WHAT IS YOUR WISH?

WELL, I WAS LOOKING FOR MY LOCKER. IT'S #001XCL. BUT THEN I SAW . . .

HAM 'N CHEESE

AND ONIONS RING

'TIS THE LOCKER OF THE KING.

OK, HOW'D YOU KNOW MY LAST NAME?

CHICKEN PATTY

AND MACAROONS

BE FOREWARNED, A BATTLE LOOMS.

A BATTLE? WHAT?

CREAM OF CORN

BROCCOLI SPEARS

WHAT YOU SEEK IS WHAT HE FEARS.

WHO?

TRUE OF HEART A CHAMPION BE.

THE SOUP OF PEA.

DRINK OF THIS,

DID YOU SAY *PEE?* NO THANKS. I BETTER GO.

I DON'T...?

THAT'S THE *BUSTED* LOCKER I SHOWED YOU THAT NOBODY CAN OPEN. THE ONE WITH THE RHYMING GRAFFITI ON IT.

I HEARD IT'S *CURSED*. THIS KID, TERRY WHITE, HAD THAT LOCKER. HE TRIED TO OPEN IT. AND THAT WAS THE LAST ANYBODY EVER SAW HIM. I THINK IT'S A *DIMENSIONAL PORTAL* TO A BARREN WASTELAND.

TERRY MOVED TO NEW JERSEY.

WHATEVER.

THIS IS *TOO COOL!* WAIT TILL EVERYONE FINDS OUT!

NO, DON'T! IT'S JUST A STUPID LOCKER.

BUT IF YOU OPEN IT, YOU'LL *RULE* THE SCHOOL.

JOIN FUTURE LEADERS

AND IF I CAN'T?

THEN YOU'LL CARRY YOUR BOOKS AROUND ALL YEAR.

WHAT'S YOUR NEXT CLASS?

SCIENCE WITH . . .

THE MAIN OFFICE. I'M ALSO YOUR FACULTY ADVISOR. WHAT TOOK YOU SO LONG?

I GOT LOST. THERE WERE THESE THREE . . .

OH, YOU MET THE LADIES OF THE LUNCH.

YEAH, THEY'RE KIND OF . . .

WEIRD? RIGHT. HAIRNETS ARE TOO TIGHT, IF YOU ASK ME. THEY SAY THEY SEE THE *FUTURE* BY READING THE LUNCH MENU.

LIKE TODAY FOR INSTANCE: CHICKEN PATTY AND MACAROONS.

BE FOREWARNED, A BATTLE LOOMS.

REALLY? I'M GLAD I BROUGHT MY LUNCH. NOW WHERE WAS I?

RAAWK! POP QUIZ!

THANK YOU, OBERON.

I DID TELL YOU YOU'D BE *TESTED*.

41

DANGER! *RAAWK!*

KNOCK KNOCK

MR. MERLYN.

IS THIS A DAGGER I SEE BEFORE ME?

MAY I SPEAK TO YOU FOR A MOMENT? IN *PRIVATE*.

YES, OF COURSE. BUT, I WANT YOU TO KNOW I HAD NO IDEA ABOUT THE PIZZAS.

MR. MERLYN, YOU'VE BEEN HERE EIGHT YEARS.

NINE, I'VE BEEN HERE *NINE* YEARS.

WHATEVER. WHAT I'M TRYING TO SAY IS, DON'T YOU THINK A MAN OF YOUR *UNIQUE* ABILITIES WOULD BE MUCH BETTER SERVED AT ANOTHER SCHOOL? *A SCHOOL FAR, FAR AWAY.* IN ANOTHER DISTRICT.

I GET YOUR POINT. YOU WANT TO GET *RID* OF ME.

NO.

YES.

DON'T BE A *FOOL*, MERLYN. IT'S NOT THAT WE DON'T GET ALONG, BUT RIGHT NOW I *RULE* CAMELOT. THINK OF YOUR FUTURE . . .

I AM.

MY *FUTURE* IS TIED TO *THEIR FUTURE*. AND I'M STAYING HERE. SORRY TO DISAPPOINT YOU.

HMMF. BY THE WAY, YOU'VE BEEN ASSIGNED *LUNCH DETENTION* THIS WEEK.

AGAIN?

THE MENU WAS RIGHT.

A BATTLE *DOES* LOOM!

HEY, GUYS!

DID YOU TELL *EVERYBODY?*

NOOO. NOT *EVERYBODY.* JUST A COUPLE KIDS IN THE LIBRARY, A FEW IN GYM CLASS AND A HANDFUL IN STUDY HALL.

OPEN IT!

YEAH!

WE WANNA SEE THE *SKELETON!*

WHAT DO I *DO?*

TRY TO OPEN IT. IT'S YOUR LOCKER.

IF YOUR HEART BE TRUE AND FINE, TURN THE DIAL LEFT TO 9.

27 TO THE RIGHT, GIVES THE OWNER STRENGTH AND MIGHT.

LEFT AGAIN TO NUMBER 3, A KING TO ALL THE STUDENTS BE.

OK.

DON'T TOUCH THAT LOCKER!

IF YOUR HEART BE TRUE AND FINE,

TURN THE DIAL LEFT TO NINE.

TWENTY-SEVEN TO THE RIGHT,

001 XCL

GIVES THE OWNER STRENGTH AND MIGHT.

LEFT AGAIN TO NUMBER THREE,

A *KING* TO ALL THE STUDENTS BE.

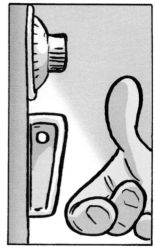

IF ANYONE THINKS THEY CAN BEAT ME, *STEP RIGHT UP!*

AS FOR YOU, YOU THINK YOU'RE *FUNNY?* THINK YOU CAN MAKE ME LOOK *STUPID?* I'M GONNA *BOUNCE* YOU LIKE A DODGEBALL.

NOBODY MESSES WITH *JOE ROMAN.*

WAIT! LET HIM GO! LET'S SETTLE THIS A DIFFERENT WAY. HOW ABOUT DODGEBALL? OUR TEAM AGAINST *THE HORDE.*

HUH? WE'LL KILL YOU. WE'RE *UNDEFEATED*.

OK, BUT IF WE WIN, YOU HAVE TO LEAVE US ALONE.

AND WHEN *WE* WIN, HE SHOWS ME HOW TO OPEN THIS LOCKER, AND I PROVE ONCE AND FOR ALL THAT *I* RULE THIS SCHOOL.

DEAL.

YOU HEARD THE GEEK! *DODGEBALL MATCH*, FRIDAY AFTER SCHOOL, *GEEKS* AGAINST *THE HORDE*, WINNERS RULE THE SCHOOL!

WHAT DID YOU DO *THAT* FOR?

I SAVED YOUR LIFE. BESIDES, YOU'RE A *DODGEBALL LEGEND*, RIGHT? YOU WERE ALL-STATE, FIRST TEAM.

YOU WERE *ALL-STATE?* IS THAT GOOD?

FINALLY, WE'RE GONNA GET EVEN WITH THE HORDE!

LISTEN, ACTUALLY I WAS . . .

DUDE, I'M *STARVING.*

WE'LL HAVE TIME TO DISCUSS THIS AT LUNCH.

LUNCH, THAT'S RIGHT, I DON'T HAVE ONE.

WHAT'S THIS?

WHERE'D *THIS* COME FROM?

GREETINGS, ARTHUR OF CORNWALL. YOU HAVE MADE QUITE A NAME FOR YOURSELF.

WELL . . .

DUDE! *YOU RULE!* EVERYBODY IS TALKING ABOUT YOU!

WHERE DID YOU GET THE LUNCH?

I FOUND IT IN THE LOCKER.

ANY GOOD?

YEAH, BALONEY ON WHITE. NO CRUST, NO MUSTARD.

THE *LOCKER* CUTS OFF YOUR *CRUST?* TRADE YA!

LOOK, I DON'T WANT TO DO THIS.

FINE. IT'S ONLY A BALONEY SANDWICH.

NO, I MEAN THE DODGEBALL GAME.

ARTIE, FOR YEARS THE HORDE HAS BEEN *PUSHING* US AROUND. THEN YOU SHOW UP AND EVERYTHING CHANGES. WE'VE BEEN WAITING FOR SOMEONE LIKE YOU. WE CAN *BEAT* THEM. I KNOW IT.

BUT I'M JUST . . .

YOU'RE LIKE THAT CHOSEN ONE GUY. YOU MADE JOE EAT SOAP, YOU TRIPPED DAGGER, YOU GOT MY GAME BOY BACK AND YOU OPENED THE CURSED LOCKER.

YOU, MY FRIEND, ARE THE CHOSEN ONE, THE LEGEND.

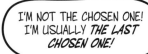

I'M NOT THE CHOSEN ONE! I'M USUALLY *THE LAST CHOSEN ONE!*

WHAT DO *YOU* THINK, MR. MERLYN?

SPORTS

WIZARDS BEAT CAVS

THE NEXT MORNING

SORRY I HAD TO WORK LATE, KIDS. HOW WAS YOUR FIRST DAY?

GREAT, MOM! I'VE ALREADY GOT *CHEERLEADING* TRYOUTS TODAY.

THAT'S *TERRIFIC*, MORGAN. WHAT ABOUT YOU, ARTIE?

I DON'T LIKE CHEERLEADING.

HA HA VERY FUNNY, YOU KNOW WHAT I MEANT.

ARTIE'S PLAYING IN A BIG *DODGEBALL* GAME ON FRIDAY!

IS THIS TRUE? THIS FRIDAY? I'LL BE THERE.

I'M *SOOO* PROUD OF YOU. JUMPING RIGHT BACK ON THE HORSE.

58

I'LL SEE YOU TONIGHT. GOOD LUCK WITH THE TRYOUTS, MORGAN.

THANKS, MOM. BYE-BYE.

WARTIE, WHAT ARE YOU DOING?

Valiant Flakes

TRYING TO EAT MY CEREAL.

NO, I MEAN TELLING EVERYONE YOU'RE A DODGEBALL STAR. *AS IF!*

I BETTER GET MY DIARY BACK BECAUSE IF I DON'T?

I'M GONNA TELL *ALL* YOUR LITTLE FRIENDS THAT YOU'RE REALLY A DODGEBALL *LOSER.*

UH . . . WHAT'S THIS?

MISSING TARANTULA

SWEET! YOU MADE POSTERS? THANKS!

I DIDN'T MAKE THEM. I FOUND THEM, IN THE LOCKER.

THIS LOCKER? THE *MAGIC SANDWICH* LOCKER?

UH-HUH.

YEAH, RIGHT.

ANYWAYS, WAYNE AND I THINK IT WOULD BE A GOOD IDEA IF WE HAD A DODGEBALL PRACTICE.

PRACTICE!?

IF TRUE AND FINE, TURN THE DIAL LEFT TO 9.

27 TO THE RIGHT, GIVES THE OWNER STRENGTH AND MIGHT.

LEFT AGAIN TO NUMBER 3, A KING TO ALL THE STUDENTS BE.

I KNOW, *YOU* DON'T NEED IT. BUT *WE* DO.

YEAH, BUT . . .

BESIDES, MAYBE YOU CAN TEACH US A FEW MOVES.

OK, BUT . . .

COOL! I'LL TELL WAYNE! THANKS AGAIN FOR THE POSTERS. I'LL GO HANG THEM UP!

AW, FISH STICKS, I'M *DOOMED.*

ARE YOU OK?

NIGHTS?

WHAT? EVERY TEAM NEEDS A NAME. SOMETHING COOL LIKE THE *KNIGHTS*.

AS IN . . . DAYS AND NIGHTS?

AS IN . . . KNIGHTS OF THE VALIANT BLADE.

YOU LIKE THE VALIANT BLADE? ME, TOO!

WHATCHA GOT THERE?

UH, OH, POSTERS TO FIND A MISSING HANNIBAL. I MEAN A SPIDER.

MISSING TARANTULA

CAN I HANG SOME FOR YOU?

YEAH, SURE, THANKS!

SEE YA AROUND.

RAWWK! HAIL TO THE KING!

MR. MERLYN?

WHAT CAN I DO FOR YOU, ARTHUR?

YOU KNOW I HAVE THIS LOCKER?

YES I KNOW. *#001XCL.* IT HASN'T BEEN OPENED IN YEARS. THAT'S QUITE A *CROWNING* ACHIEVEMENT.

THAT'S WHAT I HEAR. ANYWAYS, I'VE BEEN FINDING *STUFF* IN IT. STUFF THAT WASN'T THERE BEFORE.

WHAT KIND OF STUFF? *SKELETONS?* STACKS OF MONEY? DIMENSIONAL PORTALS?

NO. BORING STUFF, LIKE BALONEY SANDWICHES AND POSTERS. DO YOU THINK IT'S *MAGIC?*

HMM, NOTHING VERY *MAGICAL* ABOUT A BALONEY SANDWICH. ALTHOUGH MY AUNT BESSIE WOULD GRILL THE BALONEY FIRST AND MMM, MMM, THAT WAS PRETTY MAGICAL.

BUT THAT'S NOT WHAT YOU WANTED TO HEAR ABOUT, IS IT?

AH, NO.

BEING A SCIENCE GUY AND ALL, I DON'T KNOW MUCH ABOUT MAGIC.

BUT I CAN TELL YOU THAT IF THIS LOCKER IS LIKE MOST THINGS IN THIS WORLD, YOU'LL GET AS MUCH OUT OF IT AS YOU PUT INTO IT.

OH, OK. I WAS HOPING FOR THOSE DIMENSIONAL PORTALS OR STACKS OF MONEY.

AREN'T WE ALL, ARTHUR, AREN'T WE ALL?

WHEN I FIND THAT *LITTLE RUNT,* I'LL SMASH HIM.

WHEW!

HANNIBAL?!

WAIT UNTIL PERCY FINDS OUT.

HE'S GONE!

THE ONLY ONE WHO IS *GONE* IS YOU, MR. KING.

YOU KNOW WHAT *THIS* IS?

THIS IS *STRIKE TWO*. DO YOU HEAR ME? STRIKE TWO!

NOW PICK THIS MESS UP.

I'LL BE *WATCHING* YOU.

SO, WHERE IS HE?

HE SAID HE'D BE HERE. HE'LL BE HERE.

SORRY, I'M LATE. MRS. DAGGER MADE ME CLEAN UP ALL THOSE RIPPED POSTERS.

I THINK I SAW *HANNIBAL.*

WHAT? WHERE?

HE WAS IN MY LOCKER. BUT WHEN I LOOKED AGAIN HE WAS GONE.

TOLD YOU, DIMENSIONAL PORTAL.

YOU KNOW THAT GIRL GWEN?

GWENDOLYN LEE? WHY, YOU LIKE HER?

NO! SHE SAYS OUR TEAM NEEDS A NAME.

THAT'S NOT A BAD IDEA.

YEAH! HOW ABOUT *THE DECAPITATORS!*

THE *SKULL CRUSHERS* OF CAMELOT!

THE *PRINCIPAL IMPALERS!*

THE *HORDE SMASHERS!*

THE *DAGGER SMACKERS!*

ACTUALLY, SHE SUGGESTED *"KNIGHTS."*

NIGHTS? LIKE, NIGHTS OF THE LIVING DEAD!

KNIGHTS OF COLUMBUS?

NO, JUST *"KNIGHTS."*

THAT'S *LAME.* WE PRACTICING OR WHAT?

YEAH.

HOW SHOULD WE START?

YOU'VE GOT THE *MOST EXPERIENCE*, SHOW US YOUR STUFF.

YEAH, BUT NO RUNNING LAPS. I HATE RUNNING LAPS.

UM, OK, THIS IS A DODGEBALL. AND THE MOST IMPORTANT THING TO REMEMBER IS NOT TO GET *HIT* WITH THE DODGEBALL.

HEH-HEH, JUST KIDDING.

CAN'T YOU SHOW US SOMETHING WE DON'T KNOW? LIKE *DODGING*. CAN YOU TEACH US DODGING?

DODGING?

YEAH. SHOW US. GIMME THAT BALL AND WE'LL TRY AND HIT YOU.

UH, WE DON'T HAVE A FOURTH.

CAN *I* BE IT? I PLAY DODGEBALL WITH MY OLDER BROTHERS ALL THE TIME. I'M PRETTY GOOD.

GEE, THANKS, THAT SOUNDS . . .

TERRIBLE! SHE'S A *GIRL!* GIRLS CAN'T PLAY!

AND YOU'RE A JERK. ACTUALLY, YOU'RE ALL JERKS! I TAKE BACK WHAT I SAID, YOU GUYS AREN'T *THE KNIGHTS,* YOU'RE *THE DOPES.* I HOPE YOU GET CREAMED.

WHAT???

SHE'S A *GIRL*. IT'S A KNOWN FACT, GIRLS *CAN'T PLAY* DODGEBALL.

AND YET YOU'RE A *MORON*, BUT WE LET YOU PLAY.

GWEN HAS A POINT. WE NEED A *FOURTH*.

NO PROBLEM, I GOT AN IDEA!

THIS CAN'T BE GOOD.

IN A VIDEO GAME, WHEN YOU'RE *STUCK*, WHAT DO YOU DO?

GET THE CHEAT CODE?

THIS IS TRUE. BUT WHAT IF YOU CAN'T FIND THE CHEAT CODE? YOU *HIRE* A MERCENARY.

A *DODGEBALL MERCENARY?*

HERE WE GO.

YOU KNOW ONE?

YES, WE GET *SCOTT SAVAGE*. MY BROTHER IS FRIENDS WITH HIM.

THAT'S THE *LAMEST* IDEA EVER!

I DON'T HEAR YOU COMING UP WITH A BETTER ONE, "MR. LET'S-CHALLENGE-THE-HORDE-TO-DODGEBALL."

WHO'S SCOTT SAVAGE?

HE'S THE *TOUGHEST* KID IN TOWN! I HEARD THAT EVEN JOE IS AFRAID OF HIM.

REALLY?

SCOTT IS A *PSYCHO!* I HEARD HE CARRIES A KNIFE.

I GOT A JACKKNIFE IN BOY SCOUTS.

HE DOES MORE THAN *WHITTLE* WITH HIS.

OH. MAYBE WE SHOULDN'T GET THIS GUY.

THINK ABOUT IT. GOT TO GO, I'M LATE FOR DINNER.

SOMETHING TELLS ME THIS IS A *BAD IDEA.*

I'M NOT SURE I KNOW WHAT YOU ARE TALKING ABOUT, MR. MERLYN.

I'M TALKING ABOUT A *LITTLE WAGER*. ARE YOU AWARE OF A CERTAIN DODGEBALL GAME ON FRIDAY BETWEEN THESE BOYS AND ANOTHER GROUP, JOE'S HORDE?

DODGEBALL? *YES*, HMMM. YOU SAY THESE THREE AGAINST THE HORDE? PLEASE, TELL ME MORE.

IF *THE HORDE* WINS, INSTEAD OF THESE GUYS GETTING EXPELLED, *I'LL QUIT.*

REALLY? MY, MY, THAT IS TEMPTING. AND IF THEY SHOULD SOMEHOW WIN?

ARTHUR, WAYNE, PERCY AND I STAY, AND YOU MUST WEAR A *GORILLA SUIT* TO SCHOOL.

DEAL! I'LL HAVE THE EXIT PAPERS READY FOR YOU TO SIGN.

I'LL RENT THE GORILLA SUIT.

I DON'T THINK I'VE EVER SEEN HER SO HAPPY.

MR. MERLYN, THANKS, BUT WE DON'T WANT YOU TO QUIT.

NEITHER DO I. BUT I HAVE *FAITH* IN YOU, ARTHUR. BESIDES, THEY TELL ME YOU'RE A DODGEBALL LEGEND.

BUT THE HORDE *CHEATS!*

NOT THIS TIME! I'LL BE ONE OF *THE REFS.*

WHAT DO WE DO *NOW?*

WE GO GET SCOTT SAVAGE.

YEAH!

AFTER SCHOOL

I HOPE THERE'S SOMETHING TO *EAT* IN HERE, I'M STARVING.

ALRIGHT!

GEE, THANKS.

YOU READY?

I GUESS SO.

SO, WHERE DO WE FIND THIS SCOTT KID?

DUDE, HE RULES *ARCADIA*.

83

BEHOLD, ARCADIA. YOU WILL NEVER FIND A MORE *WRETCHED HIVE* OF *SCUM* AND *VILLAINY.*

STAY HERE. I'LL GO FIND SCOTT.

LOOK HOW *OLD* THESE GAMES ARE.

WHOA! IS THAT SAVAGE BLADES? I *LOVE* THAT GAME.

WOW! COOL!

I'M PLAYING THAT GAME!

SORRY.

I'LL SHOW YOU WHO'S SORRY.

NO FIGHTING IN ARCADIA.

SORRY, ANGUS. I WAS JUST LEAVING.

I AM *THE GAME-KEEPER.*

YOUR FRIEND TELLS ME YOU WISH TO SEE SCOTT.

YES, WE'D LIKE TO . . .

THERE IS ONLY ONE WAY TO SEE SCOTT. YOU FIRST *DEFEAT* HIS CHAMPION.

WHO'S THAT?

ME.

arcadia
ANGUS

DEFEAT YOU!? I THOUGHT THERE WAS NO FIGHTING IN . . .

NOT FIGHTING. YOU MUST *BEST ME* IN MY FAVORITE GAME.

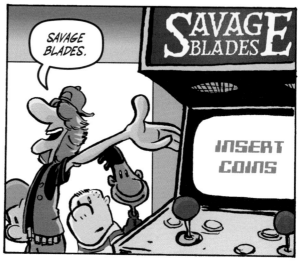

SAVAGE BLADES.

SAVAGE BLADES

INSERT COINS

PLAYER 1

PLAYER 2

KLANG

THIS IS *TOO* EASY.

 I HATE KOZ! KOZ BROKE MY BIKE!

 IDIOT, I TOLD YOU WE SHOULD . . .

SILENCE!

 WHO ARE YOU!? WHAT DO YOU WANT FROM ME?

UH, EXCUSE ME, MR. SAVAGE . . . I'M ARTIE KING. WE'D LIKE YOUR HELP *BEATING* THIS GROUP OF *BULLIES* CALLED THE HORDE.

 YOU WANT MY HELP? WHAT'S IN IT FOR ME?

 UH, WE CAN PAY YOU. I'VE GOT *$10* BIRTHDAY MONEY FROM MY GRANDMOTHER. AND SOME *COMIC BOOKS*.

 WHAT DO I WANT WITH $10 AND COMIC BOOKS?

 WELL, THAT'S ALL I HAVE.

 THEN YOU HAVE NOTHING. BEGONE!

OK,
THANKS.

BUMP

SORRY
ABOUT
THAT . . .

PICK
THEM UP!

WE JUST
HAVE A FEW
MORE.

HURRY UP!

SOME ROLLED BEHIND THE GAME.

ALMOST THERE.

I GOT IT! SORRY FOR THE TROUBLE. WE'LL BE . . .

WAIT A MINUTE! MAYBE YOU DO HAVE SOMETHING I NEED.

REALLY?

HE'S GONNA KILL US. LET'S RUN.

WHERE IS HE TAKING US?

THIS LOOKS FAMILIAR.

ARE WE ALMOST THERE?

YEAH, IT'S RIGHT HERE.

ACTUALLY, IT'S DOWN *THERE.*

SEE THAT SHINY THING? THAT'S MY FATHER'S SWISS ARMY KNIFE.

IF I DON'T GET IT BACK TO HIM, I'M *DEAD MEAT.*

OK, BUT I DON'T THINK I'LL FIT IN THAT HOLE.

NO, YOU CAN'T FIT IN *HERE*, BUT I BET YOU'LL FIT OVER *THERE*.

DOWN THE RAVINE YOU WILL FIND A CULVERT. IT'S BARRED BUT I THINK YOU ARE SMALL ENOUGH TO FIT THROUGH.

GO IN THERE AND BRING BACK MY FATHER'S KNIFE, AND I'LL DEFEAT THE HORDE SINGLE-HANDEDLY. YOU HAVE MY WORD.

NOW I KNOW WHERE WE ARE. WE'RE NEAR . . .

THE *BEAST!*

HOOOWLLL

THERE'S A BIGGER DRAIN ALONG THE WAY. I'LL GET THE KNIFE AND GET OUT THERE.

LOOK ON THE BRIGHT SIDE . . .

. . . IF YOU GET *EATEN*, WE WON'T HAVE TO PLAY DODGEBALL!

OW!

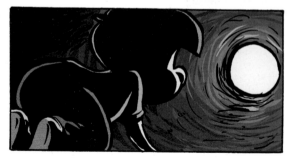

THERE
IT IS!

GOT IT!

HUH?

HOOW LL

WHOA!

AAHHHHHHA

GRRRRRRRR

EASY, BOY.

I KNOW . . .

DOGGIE SNACKS

IT'S OK. HERE YOU GO. *GOOD BOY.*

ARTIE, THANKS, I OWE YOU. I WILL HELP YOU DEFEAT THE HORDE. I *SWEAR ALLEGIANCE* TO YOU AND YOUR FRIENDS. YOU WILL NOT LOSE THAT GAME, THIS I PROMISE.

EUGENE SCOTT SAVAGE! GET IN THE CAR THIS INSTANT!

MA!?

I'VE BEEN LOOKING ALL OVER TOWN FOR YOU.

AWW, MA, I WAS . . .

EUGENE?

SEE, IT'S LIKE I SAID: NOTHING TO IT.

WITH THE COMBINATION OF MY BRAINS AND YOUR SKILLS, WE'LL GO PLACES.

YEAH, LIKE THE *GRAVEYARD.*

ARTIE, WHERE HAVE YOU BEEN? ARE YOU ALL RIGHT? WHAT IS *THAT?*

I'M OK, I JUST FELL DOWN.

HIS NAME IS *BEAST.* I RESCUED HIM. CAN WE KEEP HIM?

EWW! NO WAY AM I SHARING THE HOUSE WITH ANOTHER *FILTHY ANIMAL.*

MORGAN, BE NICE.

IT'S NOT FAIR! HOW CAN YOU LET HIM HAVE A DOG WHEN HE STEALS MY THINGS?

I DON'T HAVE YOUR *DUMB* DIARY!

LIAR!

SO, CAN WE KEEP HIM?

A DOG IS A LOT OF RESPONSIBILITY.

SECRET SECRETARY TO QUEEN MEANIE, THE OWL HAS LEFT THE NEST. OVER.

MISS FLUNKE? IS THAT YOU?

ROGER, I THOUGHT WE OUGHT TO USE CODE NAMES. OVER.

OF COURSE YOU DID. WHAT'S GOING ON?

THE OWL IS LEAVING. OVER.

EXCELLENT, YOU KNOW WHAT TO DO.

ROGER THAT. OVER AND OUT.

YOU SEEN SCOTT YET?

IT'S ALMOST FOUR.

DUDE, HE SAID HE'D BE HERE.

YO! ARTIE!

ANGUS, AM I EVER GLAD YOU GUYS ARE HERE.

WHERE'S SCOTT?

SCOTT CAN'T MAKE IT. HE'S GROUNDED. HIS FATHER FOUND OUT HE TOOK THE KNIFE. HE SAYS HE'S SORRY.

I *KNEW* IT!

BUT SCOTT TOLD ME TO GIVE YOU A TOKEN OF HIS GRATITUDE. HE SAYS YOU ARE ALWAYS WELCOME IN ARCADIA.

GEE, THANKS.

WHAT IS IT?

A TOKEN.

arcadia
land
of fun

HEY, WAIT! WHERE ARE YOU GOING? CAN YOU PLAY DODGEBALL?

I'D LOVE TO, BUT I CAN'T.

I'M GAMEKEEPER OF ARCADIA. FRIDAY IS OUR BIGGEST NIGHT. SORRY.

aracdia
ANGUS

VICTORY, DUDES.

IT'S ALMOST GAME TIME. WHO ARE WE GONNA GET TO BE OUR FOURTH?

THERE'S ALWAYS . . .

DON'T SAY IT!

HOW ABOUT YOUR BROTHER, GARETH?

YOU KIDDING ME?

I HAVEN'T EVEN TOLD HIM ABOUT HIS GAME BOY YET.

SO WHERE ARE WE GOING TO FIND SOMEONE NOW?

GIRLS LOCKER ROOM

WHAT HAS HAPPENED TO MR. MERLYN?

WHY DID WE GET THE *GIRLS' LOCKER* ROOM?

I BET MRS. DAGGER IS BEHIND THIS.

HELLO, GENTLEMEN. THE GAME STARTS IN FIFTEEN MINUTES. YOU KNOW THAT IF YOU DO NOT HAVE FOUR PLAYERS YOU WILL HAVE TO FORFEIT.

YOU ALSO WILL NEED *GYM CLOTHES*, WHICH I SEE YOU HAVE.

WHAT ABOUT MR. MERLYN?

IF HE'S NOT HERE IN TIME, WE'LL START WITHOUT HIM. HE'S PROBABLY SEEN YOUR CHANCES AND HAS ALREADY DECIDED TO LEAVE.

WE'RE SO DEAD. WE'RE *DEADER* THAN DEAD.

WE WOULDN'T BE IF IT WASN'T FOR YOU AND YOUR *STUPID* GAME BOY!

HEY, YOU'RE THE JERK WHO *CHALLENGED* THE HORDE IN THE FIRST PLACE.

ME? WHAT ABOUT THAT DUMB TRIP TO ARCADIA?

WE GOT SCOTT TO HELP US.

WHERE IS HE NOW?

AT LEAST I'M DOING SOMETHING! YOU JUST. . .

STOP! IT'S NOT YOUR FAULT! IT'S MY FAULT.

NO IT'S NOT. YOU'RE OUR ONLY CHANCE AT WINNING.

YOU'RE THE DODGEBALL LEGEND.

NO I'M NOT!

QUIT? ARE YOU KIDDING?

AFTER ALL WE'VE BEEN THROUGH?

NO WAY! YOU MAY STINK AT DODGEBALL, BUT WE'RE IN THIS TOGETHER. BESIDES, YOU'RE STILL THE *CHOSEN GUY* WITH THE LOCKER.

AS MUCH AS I HATE TO SAY IT, HE'S RIGHT. YOU'RE THE CHOSEN GUY.

THANKS, GUYS.

WE STILL DON'T HAVE A FOURTH PLAYER.

THERE'S GWEN?

UH-UH, I DON'T WANT . . .

GET OVER IT! SHE MAY NOT BE THE PLAYER *YOU* WANT. BUT SHE'S THE PLAYER *WE NEED!*

WHAT DO YOU WANT ME TO DO WITH HIS BIKE? OVER.

LEAVE IT. GET BACK HERE AS SOON AS YOU CAN.

001XCL

HEY THERE.

NO WAY! I WILL NOT GO OUT THERE LIKE THIS!

WE DON'T HAVE MUCH CHOICE, THE GAME IS ABOUT TO BEGIN.

THEY'RE *HUGE!*

THEY'RE *PINK!*

THEY SAY *"KNIGHTS PLUMBING & HEATING."*

MY DAD SPONSORS A WOMEN'S SOFTBALL TEAM. THEY PRACTICE IN THE SCHOOL FIELD AND USE THESE LOCKERS.

IT LOOKS LIKE WE'RE WEARING *DRESSES.*

Knights PLUMBING & HEATING

I PREFER *"TUNIC."*

WE'RE *ROADKILL DEAD.*

REALLY, YOU GUYS, IT'S NOT THAT BAD.

SHE'S RIGHT. AND DON'T FORGET: *I HAVE A PLAN!*

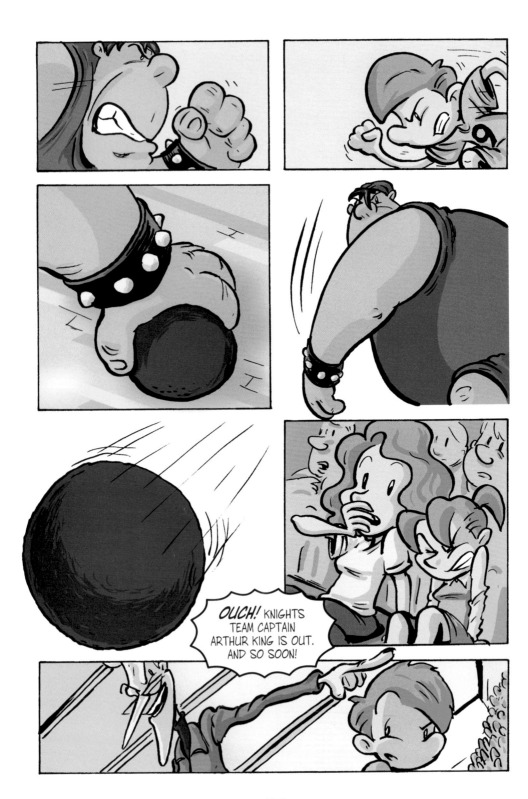

OUCH! KNIGHTS TEAM CAPTAIN ARTHUR KING IS OUT. AND SO SOON!

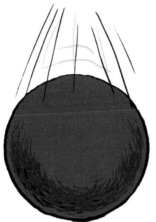

GREAT CATCH BY GWEN LEE! HORDEMAN STEWART MONK IS *OUT!*

OH, *THAT HURT.* DWAYNE FERRYMAN IS OUT! THE HORDE ONLY HAS TWO PLAYERS LEFT.

ARTHUR KING IS BACK *IN.*

OOH, NOT SO FAST!

THE HORDE IS TEAMING UP ON GWEN NOW. IT DOESN'T LOOK GOOD FOR THE KNIGHTS.

STAY BEHIND ME. MOVE WHEN I MOVE.

NOW!

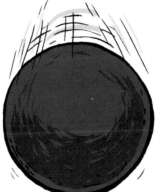

WAYNE KOZLOWSKI HAS BEEN HIT IN THE HEAD. JOE ROMAN SHOULD BE OUT.

HEY! HE HIT ME IN THE HEAD.

DON'T BE A CRYBABY.

UNBELIEVABLE! THE REF IS CALLING KOZLOWSKI OUT! GWEN LEE IS LEFT THERE ALONE. WHAT ARE THE KNIGHTS GOING TO DO?

Knights
PLUMBING & HEATING

TIME-OUT!

GWEN, YOU'RE DOING A GREAT JOB!

I NEED YOU TO GET ME BACK IN THERE.

IT'S *RISKY.* I'LL HAVE TO PUT THE BALL DOWN AND TRY TO CATCH ANOTHER ONE.

WHAT IS SHE DOING?

GWEN LEE HAS *PUT DOWN* THE BALL. THIS IS *SUICIDE.*

MONDAY

WHAT ARE YOU *LAUGHING* AT?

HEE-HEE HEE-HEE HEE-HEE

STOP LAUGHING!

DETENTION FOR YOU!

AND YOU . . .

AND YOU . . .

YOU . . .

AND YOU . . .

WHO WANTS TO PLAY DODGEBALL?

Dodgeball legend Frank Cammuso is a three-time recipient of the Wedgie. He has also received the prestigious Noogie and the Hurtz Donut.

Cammuso is the Eisner-nominated creator of the Max Hamm, Fairy Tale Detective graphic novels. He draws political cartoons for *The Post-Standard* and his work has appeared in *Newsweek*, *The New York Times*, *The Washington Post*, and *USA Today*. He lives with his wife in Syracuse, New York.